Let's Weave Color into Baskets

Pat Laughridge

Title page: *A collection of baskets—all of them made with the techniques explained in this book.*

Diagrams by permission of ACP Inc.

Basketmakers represented: Sally Benson, Suzy Boswell, Drema Clemens. Roger Clemens, Sanda Dobbin, O.B. Gardner, Velma Hart, Mary A. Jackson, Jim Laughridge, Pat Laughridge, Helen Mitchum, Vernon Naile, Melvin Smith, Jean Swing, Patricia Yunkes and ACP employees.

Printed in the United States of America. ISBN: 0-88740-056-6. Published by Schiffer Publishing Ltd. 1469 Morstein Road, West Chester, Pennsylvania 19380. This book may be purchased from the publisher. Please include $1.50 postage. Try your bookstore first.

Contents

Three dear friends made this book possible. Each of them gave me a basket, fashioned with love and skill. Later, they generously agreed to share their expertise with me and—through me—with you.

THANK YOU—
Jean Swing for the Market Basket
Drema Clemens for the House Basket
Helen Mitchum for the Field Basket

I'm also grateful to these talented friends—
Betty Sedberry for diagrams
Wayne Hinshaw for photographs

And finally for the greatest gift of all, their unconditional love and support, I thank my family—

Jim, my husband, and our daughters, Julie, Jamie, and Suzy.

Basketry Dyes

COLOR can add a whole new dimension to the design of a basket. American Indians created intricate patterns with color in their traditional coiled baskets. The antique baskets of the Appalachian region, however, were seldom dyed. They were functional items, made by hard-working people, and designed to be used daily in the home or field. Generally the baskets were left the natural color of the raw wood splint and when they were dyed, walnut hulls and oak bark—natural shades of brown—were used. The weathered look that we admire in many antique baskets are actually a product of the ageing process.

Natural Dyes

Natural dyes such as walnut hulls and oak bark are still available to those who wish to use them. Other natural dye sources are goldenrod and marigold blossoms, blackberries, poke-berries, wild grapes, and onion skins. The material to be dyed is first treated with a mordant—that is, immersed in a solution which prepares it for greater color absorption. The dye source material is crushed, soaked, boiled, and strained. Then the actual dyeing process can begin.

Obviously, gathering and preparing these materials can be very rewarding, but—like finding the right oak or ash tree and making your own splints—it is a time-consuming skill. Those who do it deserve our admiration but is there another way for the rest of us? Indeed there is!

* Is it safe to serve food in a basket which has been dyed?

Yes, if the basketweaver has used a packaged dye that is non-toxic. No if you are uncertain of the dye source. Some of the natural dyes are poisonous.

* Can I paint or stain my basket?

Yes. Reed is a form of wood, and many people have used wood stains and paints very effectively. The stains usually must be thinned with turpentine which is very hard on the reed. Paints, or even laquer, can be applied to finished baskets, but this seals the material and tends to make it very brittle.

Chemical Dyes

Just as pre-cut reed has proven to be a good material for making baskets, chemical basketry dyes are gaining widespread acceptance as an excellent way to color them. Formerly, chemical dyes required prolonged soaking in very hot water. This tended to break down the fibers in the reed and make it extremely hairy. The use of fabric dyes such as Rit became a short-cut step for many basketmakers.

Recognizing the need for dyes designed especially for use with reed, new products have been created. Most basketry dyes now available from craft shops and basketry supply houses are non-toxic. (Toxicity is sometimes a problem with natural dyes.) The new basketry dyes are extremely easy to prepare in either large or small quantities. Best of all, only five to ten minutes in the dye bath is required, and the water need not be hot. This means that the reed has been subjected to no abuse whatsoever, since it would be soaked before using anyway. Quite a variety of colors, most of them resembling nature's own subtle shades, are available. The palette on the back cover shows some of the colors which are offered by basket supply firms. In this book, we will be referring to their trade names—Indigo Blue, Leaf Green, Wood Rose, Pokeberry Red, Wild Grape, Goldenrod Yellow, Sumac Grey, and Walnut Brown. The names in some cases suggest the ultimate source, but they are categorized as chemical rather than natural dyes since they are assembled in a laboratory under controlled conditions. Nevertheless, nature will be the final determining factor in the color of your reed! The size, cut, and condition of the reed affects the degree of dye absorption. For example, small round reed dyes beautifully, but large round reed tends to resist the color. Flat reed in almost all widths dyes well, but the thickness of the reed will cause the shades to vary. Be prepared for these differences, and experiment. If you want a deeper shade, try more dye and less water, or hotter water. Additional time in the dye bath does not seem to make an appreciable difference. Experiments show that the material absorbs the color in the first ten minutes. The final color will always be a shade lighter than it appears in the dye bath.

BETTY SEDBERRY

* Will the dyed reed in my basket bleed on the natural reed if I get it wet?

No, not if you use two things:

1. Dyes which include salt or some substance to set the color.

2. Common sense! Working with freshly dyed reed which is dripping wet is asking for trouble. Use a paper towel to remove excess moisture before you weave.

If you are using a basket (either dyed or natural) as a planter, it should have a plastic liner.

One more word about color-fastness: don't take chances with RED. Remember the last time you washed a "color-fast" red T-shirt with white T-shirts? Red reed is just as unpredictable.

Getting ready to dye full hank of reed—Blue dye bath

Hank loosened—Putting into pail.

Dyeing a Full Hank

Dyeing reed does not have to be a difficult task—messy, yes, but not difficult. Wear old clothes and rubber gloves. If you are dyeing full hanks of reed or a large finished basket, the yard is the best place to work. Use large plastic pails and have the garden hose nearby. My technique is this: I go in the house and dissolve the dye in a small jar full of hot water. Outside again, I put this mixture in the pail and add water from the hose. Then I loosen the coil of reed (if it is tightly wound) and submerge it in the dyebath. (The newer basketry dyes require only five to ten minutes.) After the allotted time, I rinse the reed thoroughly with the hose. You can hang the dyed reed over a porch railing or a clothesline to dry. If you plan to use it within 24 hours, you may put it in a plastic bag—still slightly damp—and it will be just right for weaving without re-soaking. Otherwise, dry it thoroughly before storing and re-soak when ready to use.

Dyeing hank in grey dye bath—

Hank immersed in dye bath

Reed that has been dyed with a product containing salt generally will not bleed. But remember, use the reed when it is slightly damp, not soaking wet. Salt will add to the color-fastness of the dyed reed, but no dyes—natural or chemical—are immune to constant exposure to the sun.

Rinsing hank of grey to match handle for an "instant antique"—(It dries much lighter—)

Mixing Dyes and Over-dyeing

As with the natural dyes, the variety of colors and shades can be multiplied with certain dyeing techniques. Two common ones are available to the basketmaker: mixing the dyes and over-dyeing—that is, taking reed already dyed one color and putting it in another dye bath. This is often done to drab a color that is too bright, or simply to change a color. Do not be afraid to experiment with these techniques even if you are not color-wise. You can try a few pieces of reed before committing the entire hank to the dye bath.

Dyeing handle in grey dye bath—

Blue and red—

Blue and red overdyed with grey

9

Kitchen Sink Dyeing

There is yet another, simpler way to add color to your basket. I call it "Kitchen Sink Dyeing," and it is as easy as dyeing Easter eggs.

Dissolve a scant teaspoon of dye in one or two cups of very hot water. Use a small plastic container that you can discard later. Dampen a single strand of reed and re-coil it to fit into the container. Submerge it in the dye bath for five to ten minutes. Rinse the strand under running water. Pat it dry with a paper towel and then put it aside until you are ready to weave it into your basket. It can actually be used almost immediately. You will be surprised at the impact that one of two rows of dyed reed can bring to your basket.

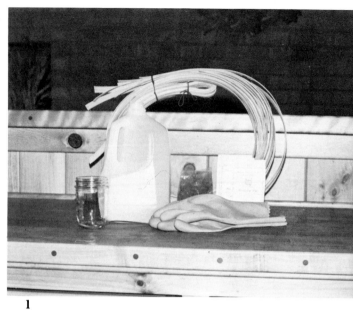

1

2

3

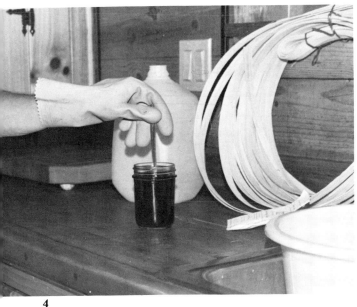

4

7

5

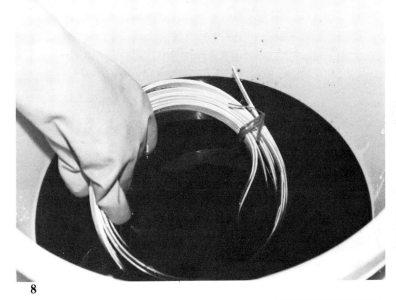

8

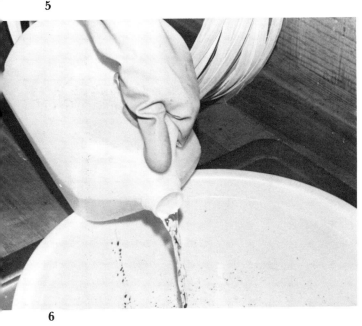

6

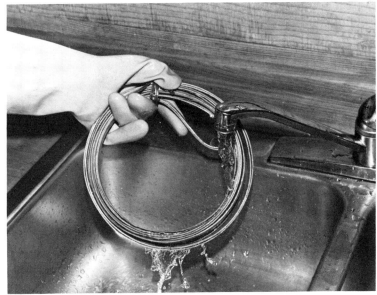

9

Dyeing the Completed Basket

You may prefer to weave with natural reed and then dye your completed basket. This can be especially effective if you wish to use brown or grey tones to get an antique look. Usually only a few moments in the dye-bath are needed for this attractive effect. A word of caution: NEVER soak handles that have been joined with water soluble glue. It is heart-breaking to invest your time and energy in a basket, only to have the handles come apart.

1

Of course, you can dye several more strands or hanks of reed before you discard the dye bath. The color will diminish with each batch, giving a lighter shade each time, but remember that using varying shades of the same color can produce a beautiful effect. Seldom, if ever, do you get the EXACT same color when dyeing reed since the size, cut, and texture of the reed all influence how the dye "takes." The dye bath may be saved a day or two if you cover it, but after that it tends to separate.

2

12

3

4

5

Thoughts Before Weaving

I've often stopped to wonder what it is about baskets that attracts our attention. Why do we find them more interesting than other containers—boxes for instance, or buckets, or bags? Is it because baskets, in a world of mass production, have maintained their individuality? No two are ever exactly alike. Behind each basket there is a real person. These individuals start with materials from the earth and add their own energy and creative spirit.

Baskets have been a part of civilization since ancient times. Some were practical; others purely decorative. In Egypt, excavations have uncovered baskets that were used for storing grain thousands of years ago. The Biblical record has also given us a beautiful picture of the mother of Moses weaving "an ark of bulrushes"—no doubt a watertight basket—in which to hide her infant son. Centuries later, field hands split slender oak trees into thin strips and wove them into large, sturdy baskets for carrying cotton. Every culture has made and used baskets for their own purposes.

In every age, resourceful basketmakers have learned to meet a particular need by using the material at hand. Their skills derived from patience and practice. Instructions were passed by demonstration from one generation to another; rarely were they written down.

It is encouraging that recent years have brought renewed interest in baskets. Today people are not only admiring them, but learning how to make these versatile containers themselves. Perhaps that is because we have discovered a wonderful secret about basketmaking. It is not a skill to be practiced only by the artisan who splits his own material and makes each basket a work of art. Neither is basket-making a super-simple skill, suitable only for therapy or mindless diversion. There is an inviting middle ground! Using natural materials and dyes which are easily available from craft shops and basketry supply houses, anyone can complete a basket that merits pride. This does not diminish the work of the skilled artisan. Indeed, it makes us more appreciative of him. This new approach allows every individual to share the joy and satisfaction of weaving a basket of one's own.

Step by step instructions for three baskets—A MARKET BASKET, HOUSE BASKET, AND FIELD BASKET—will introduce you to the materials and basic techniques used in weaving and dyeing a flat bottom basket. These three were chosen for several reasons.

* TRADITION They are reproductions of beautiful American traditional baskets.
* SIMPLICITY They are easy to make, using very basic skills, yet they are interesting enough to challenge a seasoned basketmaker.
* SIMILARITY They are all of one basic type—a splint basket with a flat bottom. The bases are all either square or rectangular, woven in a latticework pattern.
* COLOR POSSIBILITIES The design of each of the baskets is greatly enhanced by the use of color.

Color in American antique baskets was the exception rather than the rule, but now that dyeing the materials has been simplified, the addition of color is an exciting option.

More and more craftsmen have been incorporating color into their baskets. You can join them. If you prefer the traditional look, keep the colors subtle and use them sparingly. If you are making a more contemporary basket, try some of the brighter shades. Fine art work can be achieved when color is added as part of the design. Consider, for example, the baskets of American Indians, East Asians or Africans. Just remember that the important thing is to use color in shades and quantities which will enhance the basket, not overshadow it.

All of the baskets covered in this book are beautiful in their natural state. However, color can add a new dimension to the design, and—as you can see from the dyeing instructions and accompanying pictures—the process is not difficult. Your first step is to plan your basket, deciding how color will be added most effectively.

If you wish to dye the entire basket one color, wait until after the basket is completed. If you plan to add specific color accents, dye the reed before you begin. Since methods vary, ideas for incorporating color into the basket will be given before the instructions.

I know you will be proud of the baskets that you are about to make, and for most of you, this will be just the beginning. Using the techniques for weaving and dyeing which are introduced here, you can go on to make a variety of baskets of the same type. All of the baskets pictured on the title page utilize the skills which you will learn. Basketweavers have varied the sizes, shapes, details and color to come up with their own versions of colorful baskets. Soon you will be making the same kinds of creative decisions.

BEFORE YOU BEGIN . . .

1. Read the sections on materials, tools, weaving, and dyeing.
2. Shop for your supplies. A list of the basketry materials needed to complete the three baskets is included. Visit your local craft store or contact basketry supply companies.
3. Assemble your tools and materials.
4. Dye the reed in the colors you have chosen. Suggestions for adding color are given at the beginning of each set of instructions.

You are now ready to begin! It's a good idea to make the Market Basket first. Since it is the least complicated of all the designs, it will give you a chance to get used to the materials and to concentrate on fundamentals. Many of the same steps will be repeated in the other baskets, and new ones will be added. Some of the terminology may not be familiar. If you come across an unfamiliar term, refer to the glossary at the end of the text.

Market basket dyed Walnut Brown after weaving. House Basket woven with reeds dyed Wood Rose. Field Basket woven with Indigo Blue dyed reeds.

Above are the three basket shapes for which step-by-step directions are given on the following pages: top, a market basket; left, a house basket; and right, a field basket.

In the basket directions that follow, there are many suggestions for adding color. You will see how color can accentuate a pattern, "antique" a new basket, or add a special touch to a traditional shape.

16

Materials

I like to think of basketry as a local craft, often influenced by the materials of the region and the occupations and interests of the basketmakers who live there. Traditionally baskets were constructed of materials natural to a particular region. For instance, basketmakers in the Appalachian Mountains used willow, oak, ash, or hickory splints which they painstakingly cut and smoothed by hand. Wisteria, honeysuckle, and grapevines were bent into handles.

Today, since finding and preparing these materials is often difficult and time-consuming, many new basketmakers have begun using reed, which is available commercially. This material—actually the core of rattan—is an excellent substitute for hardwood splints. Rattan is a natural material, a climbing palm which grows in the tropics. The tough outer covering is removed and cut into shiny strips called *cane*. These are mainly used for weaving chair bottoms.

Types of Reed

Reed (the inner core of rattan) is cut into various shapes and sizes and is sold in units of approximately one pound called "hanks." Flat strips are cut into widths ranging from 3/16" to 1", and are called *flat reed*. Similar widths are cut with only one side flat while the other side is gently rounded. This is called *flat oval reed*. Both types of reed are identified by their shape and width. For example, you would specify "two hanks of 1/4" flat and one hank of 1/2" flat oval."

Flat Reeds

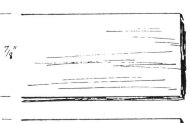

Flat Oval Reeds

Some reed is cut round and called *round reed*. It comes in a wide range of sizes, from slender as a toothpick to a heftier dowel size. The diameter of round reed is measured in millimeters, but it is usually identified by numbers beginning at 0. When ordering, you might ask for "two hanks of #6 round reed." The smaller sizes of round reed (those with the smaller numbers) make excellent weavers, as they are very flexible. The larger sizes may be used as ribs (the sturdy skeletal structure) in baskets of ribbed construction. They may also be used to smooth a top rim. Some basketmakers choose to shape the larger sizes of round reed into handles and rims.

Craft shops and basketry supply companies generally sell all of these materials in units of approximately one pound. These units are called hanks, implying that the long strands are tied together at one end. As a matter of fact, the round reed and much of the flat and flat oval now comes neatly wound into coils, but the original terms—hank, or bunch—are used to refer to a pound of reed, no matter how it is packaged!

Because it is a natural material, reed will vary in width, thickness, color, and flexibility. Certainly it should not be too brittle or hairy, but don't worry about minor variations. They will ultimately add to the beauty of the finished basket.

Round Reeds

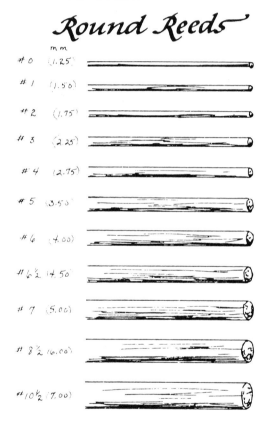

m m
#0 (1.25)
#1 (1.50)
#2 (1.75)
#3 (2.25)
#4 (2.75)
#5 (3.50)
#6 (4.00)
#6½ (4.50)
#7 (5.00)
#8½ (6.00)
#10½ (7.00)

Betty Slobberry

Another cut which is often used to form the rim of a large basket is *half round*. It is just what you would expect from the name—round reed which has been sliced in half, lengthwise. Ask for it by width, "1/2" half round," for example.

Half Round
↓
2"

Selecting Handles

If you want a handle for your basket, you will find them available ready-made in a wide variety of materials and shapes. Most commonly they are saw-cut of hardwood, but many are hand-made as well. *Round hoops* are most often used in making the traditional "Egg" or "Gizzard" basket. *U-shaped handles*, which may or may not be notched, are inserted into the sides of a completed basket. A *"D" handle* may be built into the base of a large basket to give it extra strength. The "D" gets its name from its shape—it looks like a capital letter D which has been turned so that the flat side forms the base. The "D" is also called a market handle, probably because it works so nicely in a market basket.

Names for materials as well as for techniques and basket shapes will often vary from one region—or even one basketmaker—to another. To someone whose grandmother gathered eggs in a particular shaped basket, that shape will always be an Egg Basket. Someone with different memories, seeing the same basket, might exclaim "Oh yes, that's a Yarn Basket!"

Hoops

U Shaped Handles

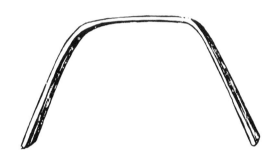

Market Handles

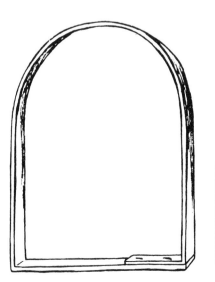
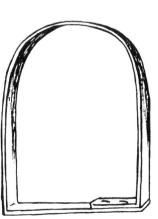

Notched Handles

Stocking Supplies

If you are a beginning basketmaker, you'll find you sometimes have to buy a hank of reed when you only need a few feet of a particular size. Think of it as if you were stocking a new pantry. You would need to buy a whole can of baking powder even though it would only be used one teaspoon at a time. As you make more baskets, you will accumulate a good stock of materials. In future instances, you may substitute from reed you have on hand. For example, if directions call for 1/2" reed and you have 3/8" on hand, it will usually make very little difference in the basket if you substitute one size for another. This is one of the things I love about weaving a basket: there is such freedom for the weaver. No two baskets will ever be exactly alike, even though they are made from the same directions by the same basketmaker. To me, this is part of the very personal charm of this craft.

Basic Materials Needed To Complete The Three Baskets

Handles - one each
   6" x 10" *market* or *D-handle*
   12" x 10" *market* or *D-handle*
Flat Reed - one hank each
   1/2", 5/8", 3/4"
Flat Oval Reed - one hank
   1/4"
An assortment of basketry dyes

Additional Materials Needed

These are listed separately because you will use only a very small portion of a hank. As you make more baskets, you will find many other uses for the remaining portion.
   Flat Reed
      1/4", 3/8", 1"
   Flat Oval Reed
      1/2"
   Round Reed
      #2, #6, #8 1/2

* How many feet are there in a pound of reed?

Before answering this question, let me re-emphasize that a unit of reed is approximately one pound. Sometimes it is a little more, sometimes slightly less. The number of feet per unit will also vary. Obviously if the reed is cut thicker, there will be less footage.

With those qualifications in mind, here is a table of approximate footage per hank in the sizes most frequently used in basketmaking. It can be helpful in determining how much reed you need for a particular basket.

FLAT REED

Width	Approx. Footage
3/16 inch	400 feet
1/4 inch	350 feet
3/8 inch	245 feet
1/2 inch	170 feet
5/8 inch	115 feet
3/4 inch	105 feet
7/8 inch	95 feet
1 inch	75 feet

FLAT OVAL REED

Width	Approx. Footage
3/16 inch	300 feet
1/4 inch	275 feet
3/8 inch	175 feet
1/2 inch	90 feet

ROUND REED

# Size	Diameter	Approx. Footage
0	1.25 mm	2000 feet
1	1.50 mm	1600 feet
2	1.75 mm	1100 feet
3	2.25 mm	750 feet
4	2.75 mm	500 feet
5	3.50 mm	350 feet
6	4.00 mm	200 feet
6 1/2	4.50 mm	160 feet
7	5.00 mm	150 feet
8 1/2	6.00 mm	100 feet

Tools

The tools needed for making baskets are mainly household items. It's nice to keep them all together—in a basket, of course!

Spring-loaded clothespins—A must! Clothespins will hold weavers or a rim in place until additional weaving secures them.

Basket awl—Tool resembling a short ice-pick. Used for opening spaces for the reed to pass through. Always work with the sharp end pointed away from you.

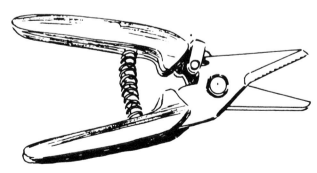

Basket reed cutters—Sharp, spring-loaded clippers which will cut all types and sizes of reed. Old scissors are not as satisfactory but they may be substituted.

Plastic coated twist-ties—(Found packaged with plastic garbage bags or on loaves of bread.) These are very helpful in securing a strand of reed when you coil it for soaking or dyeing. Avoid the paper covered ties as they will fade in the water and discolor the reed.

Tape measure—Keep it handy for measuring lengths of reed and the basket itself as it progresses.

Pencil—Used for marking the center and edges of the basket base. These marks are easily erased after the basket is underway. (Don't use a pen or felt marker!) Also handy for making notes.

Pocketknife—Used for whittling a notch in a handle or for making a neat splice on rim materials.

Pan of water—Reed is soaked before using to make it more flexible. Stakes are submerged briefly without coiling, but weavers are coiled individually and secured with a twist-tie before dropping them in the pan of water.

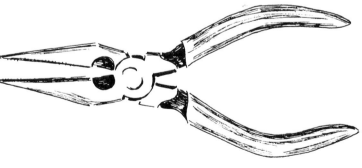

Needle-nose pliers—(Nice to have, but not absolutely necessary for making the baskets in this book.) These are used mainly when you work with small round reed as a weaver. Crimping the point where a sharp turn is to be made crushes the fibers and keeps the reed from breaking. Pliers are also helpful in pulling reed through a tight place.

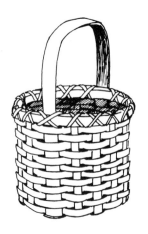

* Is it all right to re-soak reed?

Absolutely. Anytime the reed you are using begins to dry out, dampen it again. This happens most often with the piece being used as a weaver, but it may also be necessary for stakes that must be bent or shaped. One word of caution: Handles joined with water soluble glue cannot be soaked. You can probably get away with a quick dip into the water or dye bath, but no more than that!

* How long should I soak my reed?

There are as many answers to this one as there are types of reed. Anything from a quick dip to five minutes will usually suffice for flat reed if it is to be used as stakes or as weavers. Flat or flat oval reed which will be used as lashing must make sharper turns, so it must be soaked longer. Round reed needs five to ten minutes. Again, the end use determines the amount of flexibility needed.

I think the folks who recommend twenty or thirty minutes are definitely talking about oak splints. There's no doubt that reed absorbs moisture much quicker than hardwoods. Over-soaking and over-working reed causes the fiber to break down, making it hairy and stringy, so this is to be avoided. On the other hand, working with reed which is too dry is equally as bad. It will not take long for you to get a feeling for your material. It should be just damp enough to be flexible when you work.

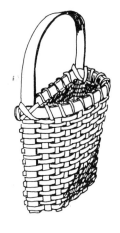

* Isn't basketmaking hard on your hands?

It does have a drying effect, but nothing that a little hand lotion can't cure. Of course, we're talking about working with pre-cut reed. If you were felling trees and making your own splints, it would be another story.

Basic Techniques

Following are general instructions for basic techniques used in weaving the Market Basket, House Basket, and Field Basket. Read through these instructions and look carefully at the diagrams. Do not be discouraged if you do not understand them completely! Understanding comes with actually making the baskets, step by step. Use these general instructions and diagrams for reference as you work.

Laying out a base with a D handle

In the instructions that follow, the number of stakes and their lengths are given. But suppose you see a basket of this type which you wish to copy, or perhaps you want to make a basket of your own design. To determine the length of the stake, *add the length of the base, plus 2 times the height, plus 8 inches.* The sum is the length of the horizontal (lengthwise) stakes. Use the same formula to determine the length of the vertical (crosswise) stakes. This is really much simpler than it sounds and the logic will be obvious to you after making only one basket!

Generally, the base is laid out in a latticework pattern, with horizontal and vertical stakes interwoven over and under each other. Mark the center crossing and space the stakes evenly from that point. If you are using a "D" handle (one which has a base structured to fit into the bottom of the basket), count the handle base as a stake.

---

* How can I distinguish the right and wrong sides of flat reed?

Sometimes you can tell the difference just by looking at it, or by running your finger across the reed. If you're still uncertain, bend a dry piece over your finger. The wrong side will tend to splinter more. Always keep the right (that is, the smoothest) side on the outside of your basket. If you are using flat oval reed, keep the oval side out.

There is one exception to the "right side out" rule. When you are forming the rim of the basket, two pieces are placed back to back over the top row. Both the inner and outer parts of the rim should have the smooth side showing.

Laying out the base

Stakes form the base and sides of a flat bottom basket. These stakes are cut from flat reed, using a width appropriate to the size of the basket. A small or medium-size basket might use 3/8" or 1/2" material; a larger basket, 5/8" to 1". The reed is measured and cut according to the directions. (Always cut the longer pieces first.)

Mark the center of each stake on the wrong (the roughest) side with a pencil. It is sometimes helpful to dampen the stakes to "uncurl" them before you mark. If you find one to be extremely crooked, discard it and cut another piece.

Blending

For a closely woven bottom, stakes may be originally positioned without the usual open space. However, some of the stakes must soon be integrated with adjoining stakes to allow the weaver to travel over and under with ease.

Blending stakes

Adding parallel filler strips to base

Filler Strips

There is another easy way to have a base without the open spaces. Lay the base out in the usual latticework pattern. After the basket is completed, use short pieces of reed, called filler strips, to fill in the spaces. Weave the strips over and under, hiding the ends under a stake at the edge of the base. If the filler strips are woven parallel to the existing stakes, this will of course give you two or more "over's" side by side.

The same technique may be used, weaving the added pieces on the diagonal. In this instance, a smaller width of reed may be used. The spaces are not filled completely, but it gives a beautiful decorative effect. Just imagine a basket with this base hanging from a beam in your kitchen!

Adding diagonal filler strips to base

UPSETTING THE BASKET

Upsetting is the tradional term for turning up the sides of the basket. It is also used as a noun—the upsett. (The noun isn't in my dictionary either. I think it must be one of those wonderful made-up words that expresses the action so well that it continues to be used.)

Always measure the base and make the necessary adjustments before upsetting the basket. The stakes should still be damp, but you may need to wet them again. Using a ruler or just your finger as a guide, bend the stakes gently upward at the edge of the base. They will not stay up by themselves at this point, so clip several of the stakes together with clothespins to hold them up. Re-position the clothespins as you weave the first two or three rows, then discard them.

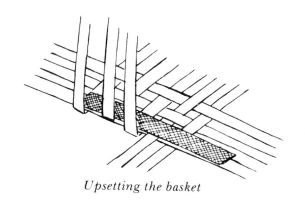

Upsetting the basket

---

* What do I do if a stake breaks?

If it breaks at the upsett, cut another one and replace it. If it should happen after several rows of weaving, trim the stake to end behind a weaver. Insert a new stake down into the weaving, overlapping the old one.

WEAVING THE SIDES

Weaving the first row or two of a basket can be very frustrating. The reed seems to have a mind of its own. Just remember that you are in charge in this battle of warp and weft, and you will certainly prove it by the third row. I think this must be why I prefer making a tall basket. It gives me more time to be in control. Once the weaving is underway, there is a wonderful rhythm to it. Over/under/over/under/over. *Randing* is the word given to traveling over and under with a single weaver. (This word is not to be found in my dictionary either, but doesn't it catch the rhythm perfectly?)

There are of course many variations on the randing theme. The Market Basket described in this book uses the simple over one/under one pattern. The two other baskets use different over/under combinations.

The three baskets also demonstrate two distinctly different weaving techniques: continuous weaving, and start and stop.

Continuous Weaving

Continuous weaving means that you continue weaving around the basket with the same piece of reed, as many rows as possible until it needs to be spliced to complete the desired number of rows. You must have an uneven total number of stakes to do continuous weaving in a simple under one/over one pattern.

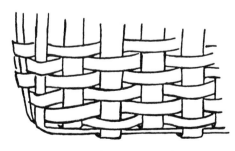

Continuous weaving

Start and Stop Weaving

Start and stop weaving means that each row is woven independently. You START with a piece of reed, travel one time around the basket and STOP when you get back to your original starting place. The reed is cut and the end hidden behind a stake. On the second row, you start and stop again, alternating the over/under pattern of Row 1. This technique is a bit slower than continuous weave, but it allows you to use different widths of reed, or even to change from flat to flat oval or round. It also gives you an opportunity to insert bands of dyed reed.

No matter which weaving technique you may be using, it is always important to take time to push the horizontal rows of weaving down closely together. Hide the splices and loose ends inside the basket as best you can. A tight, neat weave is the mark of a good basket.

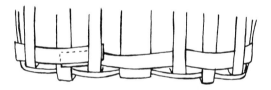

Row 1 of start and stop weaving

Three rows of start and stop weaving

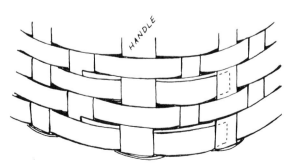

Start and stop weaving showing handle treatment and hiding the ends of the reed.

SPLICING

Splicing means joining a new and similar piece of reed to an old one which is ending. The splice should be as hard to detect as possible. With flat and flat oval reed, end the old piece behind a stake. Let the new one begin two stakes back (also behind a stake). Overlap the old piece until it ends, then continue weaving with the new piece.

Splicing flat and flat oval reed

If you are splicing small round reed that is being used as a weaver, simply lay the new piece side by side with the old one and continue weaving. The next row will lock it in place. The splice should always be on the inside of the basket.

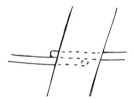

Splicing round reed

SECURING THE TOP ROW

Cutting Inside Stakes

After the top row has been completed, the inside stakes (those which are covered by the top row of weaving) are trimmed flush with the top of the basket.

Cutting the inside stakes

Tucking Outside Stakes

The *outside stakes* (those not covered by the top row of weaving) are bent into the basket. Dampen these stakes, especially at the crease, so that they will bend without breaking. You need

not worry about some splintering as this area will be covered by the rim. Bend the stake into the basket to determine the length necessary for it to slide under one or more rows of horizontal weaving and end under the next row. Mark the stake at this point and cut it, tapering the end if you wish. Now roll the trimmed stake gently back and slip it down inside the basket, under the rows of weaving. You will need to use your awl or a table knife to open a space for the stake.

ADDING THE RIM

The *rim* is added to give a smooth, neat finish to the top of the basket. Many variations are possible, but the basic idea is to cover the top row of weaving with two pieces of reed, sandwich style. You may use flat, flat oval, or even the heavier half round reed, so long as it is as wide or a bit wider than the reed on the top row.

Adding the rim

These pieces are held temporarily in place by clothespins. You will notice a small gap around the top of the basket, between these two pieces. This gap may be nicely filled with a length of round reed (usually #5, #6 or #7). If there is a handle, the reed may be cut to fit up against it, or the reed may travel outside the handle and meet with the ends neatly joined. A few slices with a sharp pocketknife will make the ends of the round reed fit nicely. This is called a *slyped cut*. Clothespins will hold the rim intact until the next step, *lashing*, pulls it all together.

Slyped cut

LASHING

In lashing, various parts of the rim are held securely together with a long, narrow piece of reed. You may use flat, flat oval, round reed or even cane, but it must be well-soaked and very flexible. The end is secured inside the basket, and the reed travels around the basket using an overcast technique. It may be single-lashed or criss-crossed. The lashing loops over the rim and threads through a hole under the rim and to the right of each stake. After pulling the reed tight, continue the pattern all around the basket.

SIGNING THE BASKET

Signing a finished basket takes very little time, but it makes the basket even more special to you in later years, or to friends and family lucky enough to receive it as a gift. A wood-burning tool is the best instrument to use to sign your initials (or name) and the date. Find an inconspicuous place on the bottom of the basket, the handle, or handle base. Or you may cut a short piece of the material used for stakes, sign it, and then slip it into the weaving inside the basket. Either way you do it, this will make a basket—especially your first one—a real treasure.

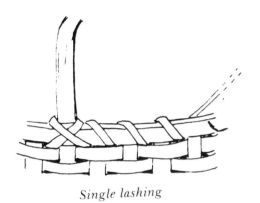

Single lashing

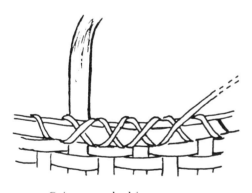

Criss-cross lashing

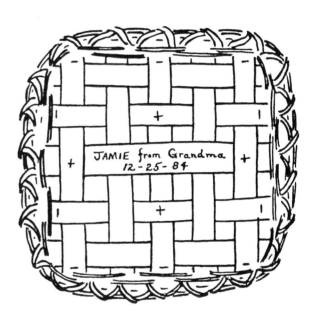

JAMIE from Grandma
12-25-84

* How should I care for my finished basket? *Dryness is the enemy. A gentle sprinkling once a year will restore the reed's natural moisture. Sometimes a light brushing is all that is needed. (Antique baskets require more specialized care.)*

Market Basket

12" x 18" base. 5" deep, handle 10" high

Market baskets come in all sizes and shapes. With these instructions, you can complete a beautiful rectangular basket—large enough to carry with you many places, and distinctive enough to attract admiring glances from your friends.

The basket shown in the picture was completed with natural reed and then immersed in a walnut brown dye bath. (This requires a large wash tub and a lot of dye!) There are two easy and economical ways to get the same effect using a smaller container and less dye.

1. "Baste" the finished basket with the dye, using an old mug, or
2. Dye the handle and all the reed to be used before you begin.

Both techniques can be done in a smaller container using less dye. The brown or grey colors which have an antique look are very appropriate.

The construction of the basket also lends itself to the addition of a few rows of colored reed. For instance, you might use natural reed for the stakes and for Rows 1, 2, 4, and 6. Dye the weavers to be used for rows 3 and 5 in the color of your choice. The lashing might be a nice accent in the same color. This kind of "Kitchen Sink" dyeing can be done just before you're ready to weave. (See the detailed instructions in the section on Basketry Dyes.)

This Market Basket is also beautiful when left natural!

ASSEMBLE YOUR MATERIALS
To get started you'll need:
A sturdy "D" handle, 12" base and approximately 10" in height
3/4" flat reed for stakes
A long piece (approximately 11 feet) of #2 round reed for twining
Later you'll need:
5/8" flat reed for weaving the sides
3/4" flat reed, 2 pieces, each 6 feet long, to form the rim (Cut these now, and put aside for later use.)
1/4" flat reed for lashing, 2 pieces, each 6 feet long
#6 round reed, 1 piece to circle the rim

MEASURE, CUT, AND MARK
From 3/4" flat reed, cut the following:
9 pieces 34" long
12 pieces 28" long
These will be the *stakes* which form the base and the sides of your basket.

Find the wrong side—that is, the roughest side—of these pieces. Mark them lightly with a pencil at the center point. Mark the center of the handle base also.

LAYING OUT THE BASE

Dampen the stakes for just a few moments. Remember to keep the rougher side up.

Begin by placing four of the 34" stakes on the table in front of you. Keep them horizontal and parallel to each other, with about two inches between each one. Now position the handle crosswise on top of them. The remaining five 34" stakes are now placed parallel to the original four, within the bounds of the handle base. The stakes at the edge of the handle should lie on top of it and the others alternately under and over. Adjust the spacing, keeping the center mark in place.

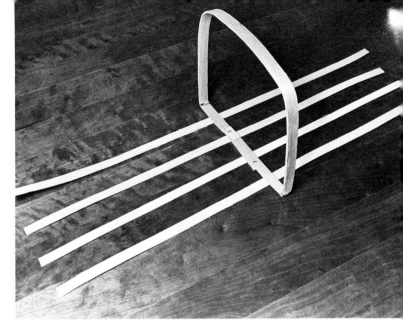

Laying out the base—Horizontal stakes and handle.

The 28" stakes are now added—six on either side of the handle and parallel to it. Weave each of these stakes over and under the horizontal stakes and then slide them toward the handle. (The stakes nearest the handle will first travel OVER the outside stake.) Allow approximately 3/4" between all of the stakes. This creates a nice latticework pattern.

Adjust the base to measure 12" x 18". (The width may vary according to the handle base.) Mark the corners lightly with a pencil.

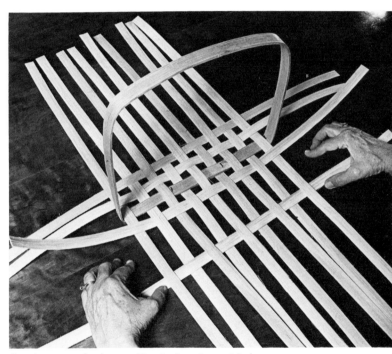

Laying out the base—Vertical stakes added. Shows "twining" in Market Basket.

TWINING

Twining is an ancient technique, basically used to draw two elements (the warp and the weft) together. One element is twisted to enclose and secure the other. There are many, many variations. In this project, we will use a very simple form of twining to secure the basket base.

You will need a long piece of #2 round reed which has been soaked five to ten minutes. The length should be a little more than twice the circumference of the base—in this case, approximately 11 feet. If you do not find a piece this long, just use the longest piece available. It can be spliced if necessary.

Bend the reed at a point an inch or two off center. Loop it over a stake—one stake past the upper left corner, and pull the ends of the reed to the right. These two weavers will now move alternately, clockwise. Begin with the weaver which is on top of the looped stake. Carry it behind the next stake. Pull it down toward you, underneath the resting weaver, and drop it. Pick up the other weaver and follow the same pattern—carry it behind the next stake to the right. Pull it down, underneath the resting weaver, and drop it. Continue this pattern, alternating weavers until you are back at your starting point. Clip both weavers, allowing enough to tuck the ends neatly in the weaving.

NOTE: If you should need to splice, just lay a new piece of reed beside the old one, weaving the two as one under at least one stake. Tuck loose ends in the weaving. Avoid splicing on a corner.

UPSETT THE BASKET

Turning up the stakes to form the sides is called *upsetting the basket*.

Dampen the base at the edges so that the stakes may be bent without excessive cracking. Bend each stake gently upward. They will not stand upright on their own at this point. Clip several stakes together with clothespins while you get the weaving underway. Move the clothespins as you go.

Upsett

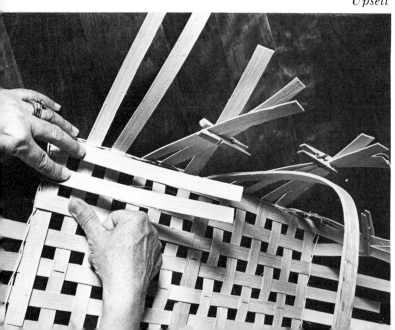

NOTE: In this type of basket where the weaving is not enclosed top and bottom, it is not necessary to pull the weaver through the warp, end to end. Simply place the weaver behind or in front of a stake by bending the stake slightly backward or forward. Cover several stakes this way and then push the weaver down in place. This moves you along very quickly (especially after the first few rows) and it saves wear and tear on the material.

WEAVING THE SIDES

The sides of this basket are woven *start and stop* which means that each row is woven independently. 5/8″ reed is used for all seven rows. Each piece, hereafter called a weaver, will need to be about 5 1/2 feet long.

Dampen each weaver just before you use it. This makes it more flexible for weaving. And remember, the smoother side of the reed should always be on the outside of the basket.

Start by placing the end of your weaver in front of the third stake to the right of a corner. The reed goes behind the next stake, in front of the next one, countinuing the over and under pattern as you move to the right, around the basket. Treat the handle as if it were another stake. (The weaver should be traveling over the handle on this row.) When turning the corners, bend the reed gently around your finger.

Beginning the first row of weaving.

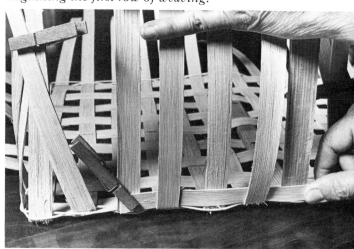

When you get back to your starting point, overlap the reed on the beginning stake. Continue to overlap, weaving behind the next stake and over one more. Then cut the weaver, allowing length enough for it to slip neatly behind the next stake. Secure your stopping place with a clothespin for the time being.

Now you are ready to start a new row. Turn your basket around so that your starting points will vary. The second row will reverse the over/under pattern of Row 1, so the new 5/8" weaver must start on a stake which the old weaver went *under* on Row 1. When you are back at your starting place, overlap and hide the end as you did on Row 1.

Ending the second row of weaving.

NOTE: The first row or two of any basket are generally the most difficult. Don't be discouraged! Use clothespins to hold the weavers in place until the basket begins to take shape. Pack the rows down as you go.

Continue weaving, using the start and stop technique, until you have seven rows. Be sure to alternate the over/under pattern on each row.

Trimming the inside stakes.
Tucking the outside stakes.

SECURING THE TOP ROW

To hold the top of the basket in place, alternate stakes are now tucked into the weaving.

First, distinguish between *inside* and *outside* stakes. Inside stakes are covered by the top row of weaving. They are trimmed flush with the top of the basket. Outside stakes are NOT covered by the last row of weaving. Bend them gently toward the inside of the basket. (You may need to dampen them at the crease to keep them from cracking excessively.)

Bend each outside stake into the basket to determine how long it must be to end neatly behind a row of weaving. Mark the stake with a pencil at this point, then trim it—slightly pointed or squared off. Now slide the stake down through the rows of weaving. Use your awl to open a space.

Adding the outer rim piece.

FINISHING THE RIM

Now you are ready to use the two long pieces of 3/4" flat reed which you cut and put aside earlier. Cut one piece of #6 round reed long enough to circle the rim. Dampen the flat reed briefly. Let the round reed soak while you begin the next step.

Cover the top row of weaving with one piece of 3/4" reed, allowing a one inch overlap. Use clothespins to hold the reed in place. The second piece of 3/4" reed is placed around the inside of the basket. The round reed, which has been soaking, is now placed between the two flat pieces to give the rim a smooth top. (Take it outside the handle.) Clothespins continue to hold all these pieces in place until they are pulled together by the final step, lashing.

Looking into the basket—as you add the inner rim piece. Adding round reed to the rim.

Note: Use a pocket-knife to whittle a smooth side-by-side splice where the ends of the round reed overlap.

LASHING

Soak two long pieces of 1/4" flat reed, each approximately 10 feet long. Anchor one piece securely inside the basket, left of the handle. Bring the reed out of the basket, over the top rim and down across the handle. Thread it back into the basket through an opening under the rim and to the right of the handle. Continue this overcast pattern, threading the reed into the basket just to the right of each stake and the handle. Pull the reed tightly as you move around the basket and discard the clothespins as you go. When you reach your starting point, trim and tuck the end into the rows inside the basket.

Complete your lashing with the other piece of 1/4" flat reed. Anchor it inside the basket near the original piece and thread it (toward you) through an opening below the rim, left of the handle. You will be moving in the same direction as before, but this time the reed will travel up and over the rim, then through an opening below the rim and left of each stake. When you have made the criss-cross pattern on each stake and handle, trim the reed and secure it inside the basket.

Beginning the lashing.

House Basket

6" x 6" base, 6" deep, handle 10" high

BETTY SIDBERRY

This little basket is a real treasure. There is a band of wide reed near the top which can be painted or stencilled with the pattern of your choice. The original basket was presented to me with a row of flowers painted on this band. The weavers (1/4" flat oval) had been dyed a beautiful shade of blue, accenting the flowers perfectly. A "bow" of small round reed sat on the handle and warm homemade cookies wrapped in a square of gingham waited inside!

To decorate your basket like the ones pictured, dye four or five strands of 1/4" flat oval and a strand of #2 round reed. The colors shown are blue and rose. The flat oval reed will be used to weave the sides of the basket. After the basket has been completed, the wide band (Row 14) may be painted or stencilled, using a harmonizing color. Fashion the round reed into a bow and attach it to the handle with strong thread.

Another alternative—one which gives the basket an antique look—is to weave with natural reed, and then immerse the finished basket in a grey dye. This can easily be done in a plastic pan since the basket is small. (See instructions for dyeing a finished basket.) Why not add an authentic antique decoration on the wide band? Outline a small, simple design on the flat side of a potato, then carve away the surrounding area so that the design is elevated. You can use a bright colored dye in a shallow container as your "ink pad." Stamp the design in the small spaces on the wide band. Hearts or apples in a bright red would be a nice touch.

ASSEMBLE YOUR MATERIALS
D Handle, approximately 6" x 10"
3/8" flat reed for stakes
#2 round reed for twining and for decoration
1/4" flat oval reed for weaving the sides, lashing the rim, and for decorating the bottom of the basket
1" flat reed for weaving rows 1 & 14
1/2" flat reed for weaving row 17
1/2" flat oval reed for the rim
#6 round reed for the rim

MEASURE, CUT, AND MARK
Cut 13 pieces of 3/8" flat reed, each 28" long. These are your *stakes*. With the rougher side up, mark the center of each stake with an X. Keep this side up while you are laying out the base.

Dip the stakes in water for just a moment.

FORMING THE BASE

Begin with one stake placed horizontally on the table in front of you. Criss-cross it with the handle at the center point. Now place six more stakes parallel to the first stake, three on either side of the handle. Slide them alternately over and under the handle, spacing them evenly. The stakes at either edge should be on top of the handle and 1/4 inch away from each side.

The remaining six stakes complete the latticework pattern when they are placed parallel to the handle, three on either side. Work each piece in an over/under pattern across the original stakes, being sure to alternate the pattern each time.

NOTE: When laying out the base and also when weaving the sides, the handle is treated as if it were another stake in the over/under pattern.

Adjust the base to measure approximately 5 1/2" x 5 1/2"—to match the handle dimension less 1/2" which will be covered by the next step.

SECURING THE BASE

Choose a piece of #2 round reed, at least 8 feet long. Soak it a few minutes or until it will wrap around your finger without breaking. Now bend this piece of reed so that one half is a few inches longer than the other. Holding it at the bend, slip the reed over a stake to the right of the handle. Begin weaving with the longer end, taking it over one stake and under the next as you move clockwise. Crease the reed at the corners to keep them square.

NOTE: Be very careful about the over/under pattern on this first row of round reed. It is easy to make mistakes at the corners and at the handle. It will help to visualize the handle extended flat like the stakes.

When you are back at your starting place, pick up the other half of the reed which has been resting and weave the next row with it. Continue weaving one row at a time, alternating the pieces of reed and always moving clockwise. Never let the second weaver pass the first one, although it may catch up. This technique is called *weave and chase*. Continue weaving around the base for four rows or until the base is square with the outer edge of the handle.

Resting weaver begins the second row of weave and chase.

Laying out the base.

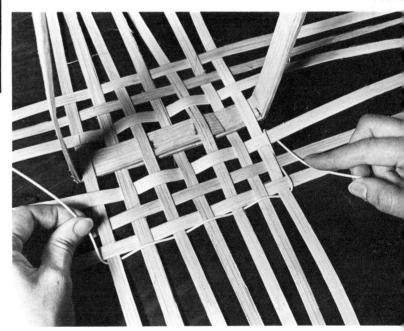

Beginning "Weave and Chase"—One end moves clockwise; other end rests.

Cutting round reed at end of weave and chase.

SPLICING ROUND REED

If your round reed should end before you complete four rows, splice it by laying a new piece beside the old one. Do this on top of a stake so that the loose end will be inside the basket. Continue with the new reed. The next row will lock it in place.

Upon completion of the final row, clip the ends of the round reed, allowing an extra inch or more to tuck into the previous row of weaving. This completes the base which should now be approximately 6" square.

UPSETT THE BASKET

First, dampen the base so that you may turn up the sides without excessive cracking. Gently bend the stakes toward the center of the basket. The stakes will not stand upright on their own at this point. Use clothespins to hold them until the first few rows of weaving are in place.

Technique Tip: Neat corners established at this point will contribute greatly to a well-shaped basket. The two stakes at each corner should always have some space between them.

WEAVING THE SIDES

(Detailed instructions follow, but use this guide for easy reference.)

Row 1	1" flat	start & stop
Rows 2 & 3	1/4" flat oval	start & stop
Rows 4—13	1/4" flat oval	continuous weaving
Row 14	1" flat	start & stop
Rows 15 & 16	1/4" flat oval	start & stop
Row 17	1/2" flat	start & stop

The first row of this basket is a wide band of 1" flat reed, woven in the *start and stop* technique. Dampen the reed for a few moments. Turn the base so that one side of the handle is facing you. START by placing the reed on top of a stake two places to the left of the handle. Take it behind the next stake and then over the handle. Continue this over/under pattern all around the basket.

(Remember—on this row and on Row 14, when 1" reed is used again, the weaver should always fall on the outside of the handle.)

When you get back to your starting place, continue weaving as you overlap four stakes. Cut the end and tuck it behind the fourth stake.

Now you will begin to use the 1/4" flat oval reed. If you have just dyed it, it will probably still be damp enough to use. If not, just dip it in clear water for a moment.

Row 2: Continue the start and stop technique, this time using 1/4" flat oval reed. Be sure you reverse the over/under pattern of Row 1.

Row 3: Repeat the pattern of Row 1, using 1/4" flat oval reed.

WEAVING ROWS 4—13

Rows 4—13 are woven with 1/4'' flat oval reed. You will be using a technique called *continuous weaving.*

Select a long strand of 1/4'' flat oval reed. Place the end of the reed behind any one of the stakes (inside the basket). Secure it with a clothespin. Weave OVER 2/UNDER 1 stake, moving to the right. When you get back to your starting place, do NOT cut the reed as before. Simply slip the reed up slightly and continue the next row with the same piece of reed.

The next row begins with the weaver traveling over both the original starting stake and the one next to it, then under 1, over 2 and so on. The pattern continues OVER 2/UNDER 1 until you have ten rows of continuous weaving.

Do not be concerned over a small gap where the second row of continuous weaving began. After another row is completed you can go back and adjust the rows of weaving to lessen the gap.

SPLICING FLAT REED

When you get to the end of a weaver, trim it to end behind a stake. Count back three stakes and place a new weaver over the original at this point. This hides both ends so that the splice is invisible. Continue weaving in the same pattern as before.

END CONTINUOUS WEAVING

Try to end Row 13 directly above your starting place on Row 4 so that your rows of continuous weaving are well balanced. Let the last row end behind a stake. Clip it, allowing enough length to tuck the end into the row below.

Row 14: Repeat Row 1. Use 1'' flat reed with start and stop weaving. Remember, this wide weaver should travel OVER the handle.

Rows 15 & 16: Use 1/4'' flat oval reed with start and stop weaving.

Row 17: Weave the final row, start and stop, with 1/2'' flat reed.

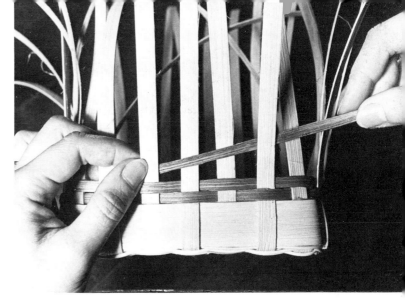

Begin continuous weaving.

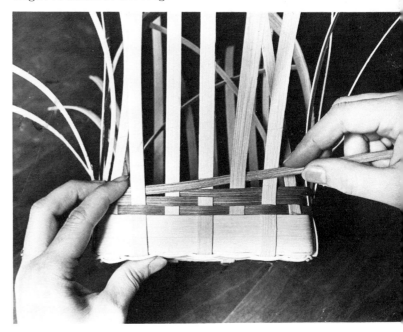

Second row of continuous weaving.

Clipping weaver to end continuous weaving.

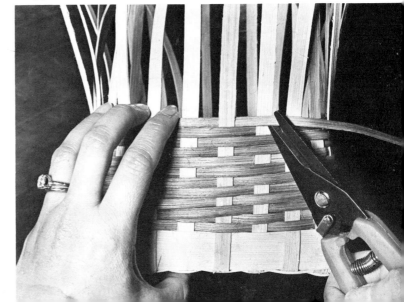

SECURING THE TOP ROW

Stakes which are covered by the final row of weaving are called inside stakes. Trim them so that they are flush with the top of the basket. The remaining stakes, which are not covered by the 1/2" weaver, are called outside stakes. Dampen them at the crease (a sponge is helpful) and bend them into the basket. Tuck them into a row of weaving. Use your awl or a table knife to open the space.

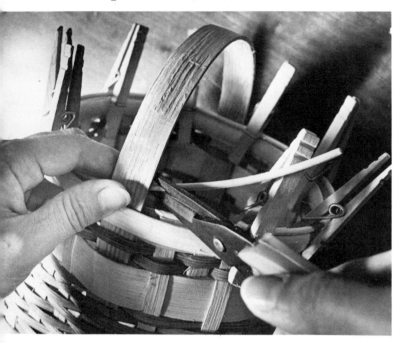

Tucking outside stakes into the basket.

FINISHING THE RIM

Cover the final row with a piece of 1/2" flat oval reed, beginning just to the right of the handle and ending with an overlap of about two inches. Secure with clothespins. Place a similar piece inside the basket to cover the same row. Now cut a piece of #6 round reed to fit between these bands of 1/2" flat oval reed. Shave the ends of the round reed so that they overlap neatly. The bands and the round reed give a smooth and sturdy finish to the top of the basket. Clothespins hold the rim together until the lashing is added.

Fitting round reed into rim.

Beginning the Lashing.

LASHING

Soak a long piece of 1/4" flat oval reed to use for lashing the rim together. Keeping the oval side up, secure one end inside the basket under the weaving on the handle. Bring it up over the rim on the right side of the handle. Make the first half of an "X" by moving down and left. Thread the reed into a hole just under the rim and left of the handle. Now bring the reed up and out of the basket on the left side of the handle. This time, moving down and to the right across the handle, you complete the "X." Thread the reed into a hole just under the rim and right of the handle. Continue this overcast technique as you move around the basket. When you reach the other side of the handle, make the "X" just as you did before. (The first stroke across the handle is again "upper right to lower left.") Continue the lashing, removing the clothespins as you go, until you're back at your starting place. Anchor the end under the weaving inside the basket.

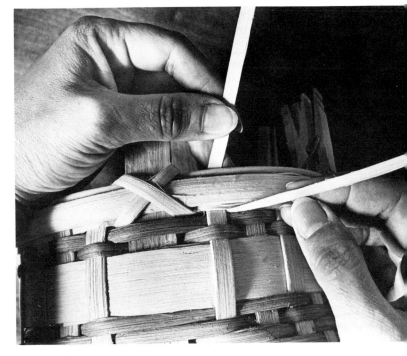

Lashing continued.

DECORATING THE BOTTOM OF THE BASKET

Using short leftover pieces of 1/4" flat oval reed, you can create an interesting pattern on the bottom of the basket. When you are doing this diagonal weaving, it is best not to dampen the reed. Use your awl or a table knife to open spaces and push the dry reed into place.

Working with the basket upside down in your lap, lay a piece of 1/4" flat oval reed diagonally across the lower left hand corner. Work it into the basket in an approximate over/under pattern. (It need not be exact since this is just for decoration.) Trim the ends and "lose" them in the 3/8" stakes. Continue working across the base of the basket, one piece at a time, in a diagonal pattern, until you reach the upper right hand corner.

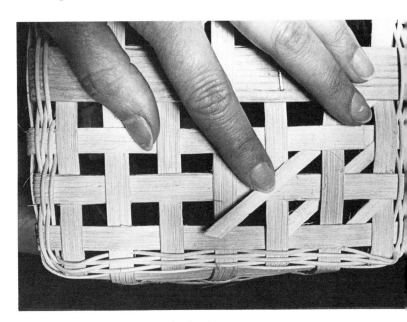

Decorating the bottom of the basket.

DECORATING THE SIDES

The 1" reed on Row 14 lends itself beautifully to extra decoration. Refer to the suggestions at the beginning of these instructions for ideas.

Field Basket

11" x 11" base, 9" deep

BETTY SEDBERRY

I love this basket! Can't you just imagine it filled with wool which is ready for spinning, or with bright red apples gathered from the tree in the back yard? It's large and strong enough to be quite useful, but its main attraction is its beauty. Color climbs up the sides in a kind of herringbone, or broken twill, pattern.

This basket is a wonderful example of the effective use of colored reed to emphasize a pattern. In the baskets shown, the 1/4" flat oval weavers were dyed one color, all at one time. (It required a little less than one half of a hank.) If you wanted to use varying shades of the same color, you could dye one strand at a time ("Kitchen Sink" method). Allow each successive strand a little less time in the dye bath. The weaving will be dark at the base, but will grow lighter as the weaving progresses.

An altogether different effect can be achieved by leaving the weavers natural and dyeing the 1/2" stakes. (Approximately one half of a hank is required.)

You might also consider dyeing the lashing for this basket. This would be a nice accent against natural materials in the rim.

ASSEMBLE YOUR MATERIALS

1/2" flat reed for stakes
#2 round reed, one long strand for twining
1/4" flat oval reed for weaving the sides
(The weaving pattern in this basket really demands that this reed be dyed. The contrasting color accents the pattern beautifully.)

Later, to finish the rim and handle, you'll need these materials:
   3/8" flat reed, one piece for the top row
   1/2" flat oval reed, two pieces for the rim
   #6 round reed, one piece for the rim
   3/16" flat oval, one long piece for lashing the rim
   #8 1/2 round reed, two short pieces (each 13") for the handles

FORMING THE HANDLES

Since the handles for this basket require several steps, it is best to get them underway. Continue the steps as you work on the body of the basket, and the handles will be ready when you need them.

Cut two pieces of #8 1/2 round reed, each 13" long. Soak for 10 or 15 minutes. Gently bend into a U shape. Tie with string to hold in place and put both pieces aside to dry.

When dry, measure and mark three inches from each end. Use a sharp pocket-knife to make a notch cut, beginning at the mark and tapering up for one-half inch toward the center. When you have made two notches on each handle, taper the ends so that they will slip into place easily. (Once they are in place, the 1/2" notch you have just whittled will be covered by an inside rim piece of 1/2" flat oval.)

MEASURE, CUT, AND MARK

From the 1/2" flat reed, cut 26 stakes, each 36 inches long. Mark the center of each piece on the wrong side. Dampen all the stakes.

FORMING THE BASE

Begin with one stake placed horizontally on the table. Criss-cross it with a vertical stake and mark the center with an "X". Now add six vertical stakes on both sides of center, leaving approximately 3/8" space between each one. Place them alternately under and over the horizontal stake. When you have 13 vertical stakes, adjust them to measure 5 1/2 inches from the center to the edge on both sides.

Now add the remaining stakes, six on both sides of center, parallel with the original horizontal piece. Weave them over one, under one, and then slide them toward center. The spacing is the same as before, giving you (approximate) 3/8" squares. Measure and adjust again. Your base should now be an 11" x 11" square.

TWINING

Twining will hold the stakes securely in place.

Choose a long piece of #2 round reed (about 8 feet). Coil the reed and soak it five minutes or until flexible. Gently bend the reed at a point an inch or two off center. Loop it over a stake near the upper left corner, and pull the ends of the reed to the right. These two weavers will now move alternately, clockwise. Begin with the weaver which is on top of the looped stake. Carry it behind the next stake. Pull it down toward you, underneath the resting weaver, and drop it. Pick up the other weaver and follow the same pattern. Carry it behind the next stake to the right. Pull it down, underneath the resting weaver, and drop it. Continue this pattern, alternating weavers until you are back at your starting point. Clip both weavers, allowing length enough to tuck the ends neatly in the weaving.

UPSETT THE BASKET

The base must be damp, especially at the edges, so that the stakes may be bent upward

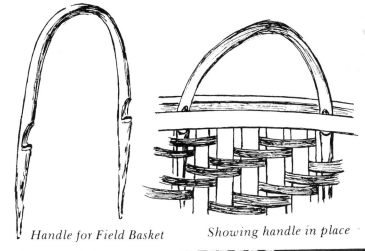

Handle for Field Basket   *Showing handle in place*

Base with twining.
Upsett

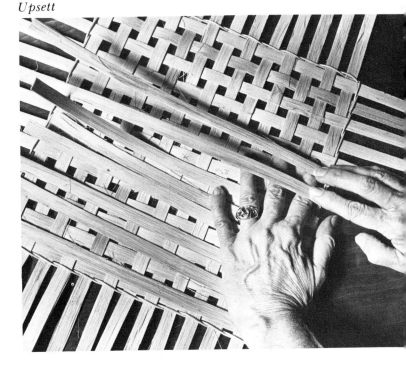

41

Market basket dyed Walnut Brown after weaving.

House Baskets woven with reeds dyed Wood Rose and Indigo Blue.   43

Starting the first row of weaving.

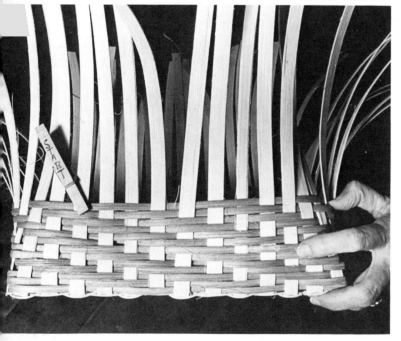

First thirteen rows, showing development of the pattern.

Beginning the final row.

without excessive cracking. Gently crease all of the stakes against a ruler or just your hand. Use clothespins to hold the stakes up for the time being. You may need them for six or seven rows.

WEAVING THE SIDES

The herringbone weave is beautiful, especially when contrasting colors accent the pattern. It requires close attention and frequent checking. If you find you have made a mistake, go back to that point and correct it. It is well worth the few extra minutes to restore the pattern.

You will be using 1/4" flat oval reed in a continuous weave. Keep the oval side out.

Begin by placing the end of the weaver behind a stake—three places right of a corner. Secure it with a specially marked clothespin. Weave over 2, under 2 around the basket. When you are one stake short of your starting place, go under ONE. Move your clothespin to mark this new starting place. Now pick up the pattern again—over 2, under 2. Keep clothespins on the corners so the weaving will not get too loose.

REMEMBER—In continuous weaving, do not cut the weaver at the end of the row. Just make the pattern signature (under ONE) and begin the next row. Let the weaver slip up over the previous row. There will be a slight gap, but this will disappear as you pack the rows down snugly.

SPLICING

When you get to the end of a weaver, overlap it with a new one. Weave the two as one until the old one runs out, then continue as before. Begin splicing behind a stake where it will not be seen, and always avoid splicing at the corners.

SHAPING

When you have five inches of weaving, begin to draw the sides in slightly. This is done by pressing the stakes toward the center of the basket as you weave.

FINAL ROWS

When the basket is approximately nine inches tall, end the 1/4" flat oval behind the starting stake. Allow one or two extra inches to tuck the end of the weaver inside the basket. As some basketmakers would say, "Lose the weaver." Isn't that a perfect description?

Pack the weaving down again to level the top row as much as possible.

Weave one final row with a length of 3/8" flat reed. Start on top of a stake and weave under one, over one all around the basket. Overlap the starting point. Clip and tuck the end behind the next stake.

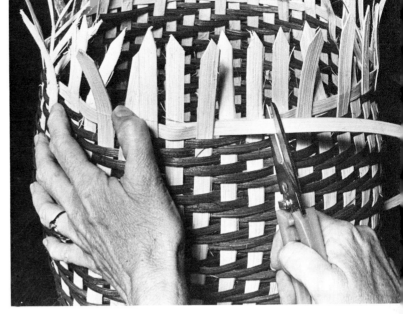

Ending the final row.

SECURING THE TOP ROW

INSIDE STAKES (those which are covered by the top row of weaving) are trimmed flush with the top of the basket.

OUTSIDE STAKES (those which are NOT covered by the top row of weaving) are bent into the basket. You will probably need to wet them again, especially at the crease. Slide the ends under a few rows of weaving.

Trimming the inside stakes.
Tucking the outside stakes.

Field Baskets woven with reeds dyed Indigo Blue and Pokeberry Red.

This picture like those on pages 54 and 55, illustrate baskets made with techniques different from those described in this book. The materials and tools are the same. This picture shows round baskets with the bases laid out as spokes.

INSERTING THE HANDLES

Find the fourth stake from a corner and insert a handle into the inside rows of weaving. (Use an awl to open a path.) The notch should be on the inside, positioned just behind the top row. The other end of the handle is inserted behind the fourth stake from the other corner.

On the opposite side of the basket, insert the other handle in the same way.

Inserting the handle.

FORMING THE RIM

After the handles are in place, cover the top row with 1/2" flat oval, overlapping one inch. (Note: Let all parts of the rim end near one handle.) Secure with clothespins. Use a similar piece of 1/2" flat oval on the inside, fitting it into the 1/2" notches so that the handles won't pull out. Place a piece of #6 round reed between the flat oval pieces to form a strong, neat rim.

Adding the outer rim piece.

Adding round reed to the rim.

LASHING

Choose a long piece of 3/16" flat oval and soak it several minutes. Turn the basket to the side opposite the place where your rim pieces overlap. Anchor the end of the reed inside the basket near a handle. Bring the reed down across the handle, moving from upper left to lower right. Thread it through a hole between the rim and the last row of 1/4" flat oval. (Use your awl to open the space if necessary.) The lashing is now brought up over the rim and down across the stake which covers the handle—this time moving from upper right to lower left, forming an "X" on the rim. Thread the lashing through a corresponding hole to the left of the handle stake. Now resume the overcast pattern (upper left to lower right) at each stake as you move around the basket to the right. Interrupt the upper left to lower right movement to make an "X" on each handle, then continue.

Discard the clothespins as you go, and pull the lashing tight at each stake. When you are back at your starting place, anchor the lashing under the weaving inside the basket.

By now this book should have some water spots or perhaps a smudge of dye here and there. That is as it should be, since it has been your companion through the making of three baskets. I hope you will be inspired to make many many more.

One thing I promise you—having made even one basket, you will never look at one quite the same again. You will find yourself examining it, counting the stakes, and mentally cataloging the techniques. You will imagine who might have made it and feel a certain kinship with that person. When you reach this stage, congratulate yourself. It means you have joined the ranks of basketlovers everywhere!

Beginning the lashing.

Lashing continued.

Basket completed!

The colors used in these baskets are identified in the smaller picture captions.

Below left: Reed dyed with Wild Grape used on alternate rows. Center: The handle and stakes were dyed Sumac Grey. Alternating bands of Wood Rose and Goldenrod Yellow are used on the sides. Right: Center bands of reed were dyed Indigo Blue—one of them was left in the dye bath five minutes, and the other two for ten minutes to get a darker shade.

Above left: Main body of the basket and the handle have been left natural. Bands of Indigo Blue and Wood Rose (all dyed in a double strength solution) have been added. Right: The stakes and two pieces for center contrast are dyed Indigo Blue. In this basket, the stakes are bent down, forming the blue rim.

50

Above left: Reed dyed Wild Grape double strength has been combined with reed dyed lightly with Wild Grape. Right: Leaf Green and Wood Rose are both used as stakes. The same colors are repeated in the center bands.

Below left: Main body of the basket and the handle have been dyed Walnut Brown. Strips of 1/4" flat oval woven in are Wild Grape, Wood Rose, Pokeberry Red, and natural. Right: The stakes and two pieces for center contrast are dyed Walnut Brown.

Above left: Weavers which have been dyed Indigo Blue are contrasted with the natural reed and handle. Right: The handle and some of the stakes and weavers have been dyed Pokeberry Red to form an interesting pattern.

Glossary

When we venture into new territory, it helps so much to know the language! The words and phrases defined here are not always found in the dictionary, and their usage may vary from one area to another. But you'll find them to be descriptive, colorful, and perfectly natural in the basketmaker's vocabulary.

Awl   Tool that resembles a short ice pick.

Base   Bottom of the basket.

Cane   The shiny outer peel of rattan, used mainly for hand caning or cane webbing.

Continuous Weaving   Using a single piece of reed for row after row of weaving.

Dye Bath   Mixture of natural or chemical dye and water.

Handle   That part by which we lift and carry the basket. A good handle is suitable in size and firmly attached to the basket.

Hank   Unit of reed, approximately one pound.

Lose the Weaver   Tuck the end of a piece of reed into rows of weaving.

Overlap   Extending one piece of material to cover another. The two are then woven as one.

Randing   Simple over and under weaving with a single weaver. In continuous weaving, this requires an uneven number of stakes.

Reed   The inner core of rattan, which has been cut lengthwise into flat, flat oval, or round strips.

Rim   Top row of the basket, usually reinforced with extra pieces for strength.

Slype cut   Tapering a round piece of reed to a flat surface.

Splice   Adding a new piece of reed when the old one runs out, usually by overlapping.

Splint (also Split)   A thin, flexible strip of wood suitable for weaving baskets or for bottoming chairs.

Stakes (also Spokes)   The warp of the basket. The upright pieces that support the weaver.

Start and Stop Weaving   Weaving each row as an independent unit. The weaver starts and then stops when a circle of the basket is completed.

Twining (also Pairing)   Two weavers entwining the stakes.

Upsett   Bending the stakes upward to form the sides of the basket.

Weave and Chase (also Chasing)   Two weavers travelling alternately around a basket in a randing weave. This can be worked with an even number of stakes.

Weaver   The piece of material which travels over and under the stakes.

Bibliography

Cary, Mara. *Useful Baskets.* Boston, Massachusetts: Houghton Mifflin Co. 1977.

Christopher, F.J. Edited by Marjorie O'Shaughnessy. *Basketry.* New York, New York: Dover Publications, Inc. 1952.

De Leon, Sherry. *The Basketry Book.* New York, New York: Holt, Rinehart and Winston. 1978.

Hart, Carol and Dan. *Natural Basketry.* New York, New York: Watson-Guptill Publications. 1976.

Ketchum, William C. Jr. *American Basketry and Woodenware.* New York, New York. Macmillan Publishing Co., Inc. 1974.

Laughridge, Jim and Jamie. *Let's Make An Egg Basket.* Salisbury, North Carolina: Kelly Publishing Co. 1981.

Miller, Bruce and Widess, Jim. *The Caner's Handbook.* New York, New York: Van Nostrand Reinhold Company. 1983.

Schiffer, Nancy. *Baskets.* Exton, Pennsylvania: Schiffer Publishing Ltd. 1984.

Stephenson, Sue H. *Basketry of the Appalachian Mountains.* New York, New York: Van Nostrand Reinhold Company. 1977.

Tod, O.G. and Benson, O.H. *Weaving with Reeds and Fibers.* New York, New York: Dover Publications, Inc. 1975.

Will, Christoph. *International Basketry.* Exton, Pennsylvania: Schiffer Publishing Ltd. 1985.

The pictures on these two pages and page 47 illustrate baskets made with techniques other than those described in this book. The materials and tools are the same, and the reader is encouraged to expand his basketmaking skills in every direction. This picture shows coiled baskets, illustrating the use of pine needles and of sweet grass.

Baskets of ribbed construction. Shown (clockwise) are a large Appalachian Egg Basket, a Hen Basket, A beautifully dyed Egg Basket, a Key Basket, and in the center a Butterfly Basket and two miniature Egg Baskets.

Index